MISCHA REVOTSKIE

I Love You Like...

POETRY FROM AN OCEANIC HEART

© 2021 Mischa Revotskie

All Rights Reserved. No part of this publication may be reproduced, or stored in a retrieval system, or transmitted in any form or by any means, electronic, mechanical, photocopying, recording, duplicating, or otherwise, without written consent of the publisher.

ISBN: 978-1-955346-06-1

10 9 8 7 6 5 4 3 2 1

Artwork by Jenny Edwards, Jill Doneen, and Shanti Albani

A special thanks to Amy for her photographic contribution to the cover.

Designed by Heather Dakota

Wyrd & Wyld Publishing
Spokane, WA

www.mischarevotskie.com

A sturdy mountain crumbles
And dissembles to the sea
A burgeoned sprout but humbles
To the wisdom of the tree
But earth will rise and trees will fall
Their girth and size beneath it all
The zephyr calms the stubborn squall
The monsoon clears the smoke-born pall

The sure foot sometimes stumbles
And finds support upon a knee
The deft hand often fumbles
And exacts recovery
The universe is sweeping
Unconceived chaotic charms
But everything is perfect
When you're sleeping in my arms

–Mischa Revotskie

Dedication

This book is dedicated to:

_____

With love:

_____

MISCHA REVOTSKIE

I Love You Like...

POETRY FROM AN OCEANIC HEART

A sturdy mountain crumbles
and dissembles to the sea
A burgeoned sprout but humbles
to the wisdom of the tree

but earth will rise and trees will fall
their girth and size beneath it all
the zephyr calms the raging squall
the weather clears the smoke-born pall

The sure foot sometimes stumbles
and finds support upon a knee
the deft hand often fumbles
and exacts recovery

The universe is sweeping
~~chaos rampant sweeping~~
unconceived chaotic charms
but everything is perfect
when you're sleeping in my arms

Preface

What happens to the mind and soul when love awakens?

What transformation?

The world lights up, even as the roots of consciousness grow deeper into the dark of mystery.

These poems reflect the love-awakening of one soul, and yet, we are sure they will resonate with all whose love is like "the calling of the spirit."

Foreword

Mischa was born and raised in the remote hills of northern California. He felt comfortable and fully himself in nature and wrote often from a place of kinship and understanding with the natural world. He was particularly inspired by the meeting of land and sea, where he penned much of his poetry.

He died in 2020, leaving his beautiful words about nature and love unpublished. He had been collecting his poems with the thought of publication, and so his sister, mother, and his beloved have brought you the collection you now hold in your hands.

Mischa's most profound characteristic was his oceanic heart. He loved truly, deeply, and compassionately. He was generous and kind. When he talked his blue eyes sparkled and invited you to be with him in these lands of delight and warmth.

His poetry came from this place of belief that love is a great healer. He embraced love generously and vibrantly, and it fed his poetry in return. He once said, "Love… whatever it asks of me."

He spent the few years before his death with his beloved, and during this time his poetry took on both a new depth and a lightness of heart. The poems in this volume are part of his promise to never stop telling his beloved of his love.

May these short expressions of love inspire you to open your heart to the gifts of loving and being loved.

From the Editors,
Shanti Albani
Jill Doneen
Jenny Edwards

April 2021

~ One ~

I love you like a waterfall
    requires open space

And spreads her beauty mistily
    upon a granite face

I love you like a hill-born horse
    enrapt with freedom's pace

Gifted with the grace of glide
    in landscape's pure embrace

~ Two ~

I love you like the slant of sun
    on rain-specked windblown leaf

I love you like a parrotfish
    takes refuge in a reef

I love you like the violin
    of a cricket's crooked haunch

I love you like the fusion
    in a moon-sent rocket's launch

I love you like the safety
    of a toughened turtle shell

I love you like the resonance
    of a monastery knell

~Three~

I love you like the upthrust
    of the mighty Himalayas

I love you like the slow descent
    of humble Mauna Kea

I love you like the lichen that
    survives in arctic climes

I love you like the sounding kiss
    of airflow on the chimes

~Four~

I love you like a melting point
    at sub-zero degrees

I love you like the final stroke
    of sunset through the trees

I love you like the cool caress
    of crystal mountain stream

I love you like the awakening
    of an ancient aching dream

~Five~

I love you like a butterfly
   flitting in the breeze

Erratic in its airy path
   but sure of where it please

I love you like a dragonfly
   majestic in its flight

Ancient in its carapace
   graceful to alight

~Six~

I love you like a church bell pealing
    The humble thrall of devout kneeling

A thunderstorm on tin-roof ceiling
    The naked tears of hearts revealing

~Seven~

I love you like the atmosphere
    invites a lost balloon

I love you like the shadow
    of a drifting sunset dune

I love you like the torrent
    of an unrestrained monsoon

I love you like the mooring
    of cloud ships to the moon

~Eight~

I love you like a pastel canvas
    beckons on the dusk

I love you like a scrimshaw carved
    requires vibrant tusk

I love you like the lighting that
    illuminates the Louvre

I love you like the deepest chord
    of an abyssal groove

~Nine~

I love you like a hummingbird
    intent upon its nectar

I love you like the preciseness
    of a pythagorean vector

I love you like an apple
    ready on the limb

Rich and ripe and redolent
    to be plucked upon your whim

~Ten~

I love you like a pendulum
    profound in oscillation

I love you like a paramecium
    requires cilliation

I love you like the warmth
    of a brand new pair of socks

I love you like the bur and mesh
    of velcro interlocks

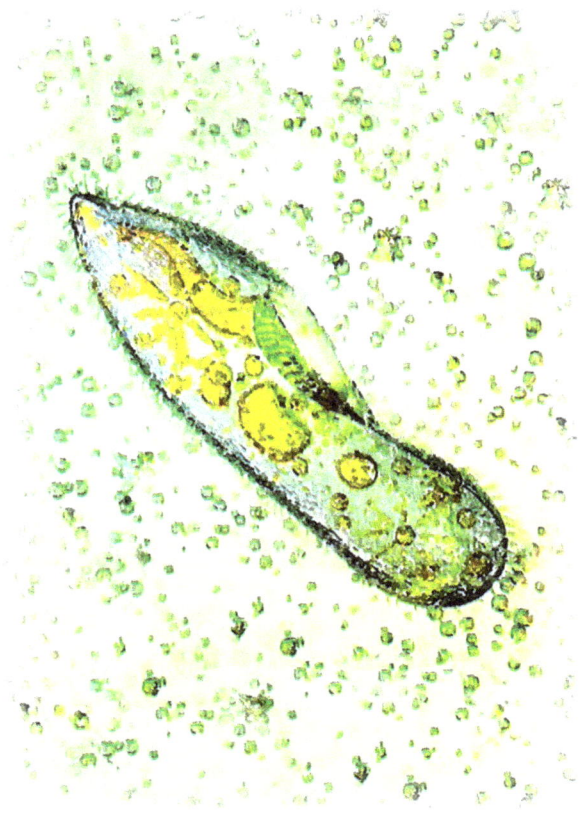

~Eleven~

I love you like the dedicated
    migration of the geese

Who formulate formation
    in V-configuration

Where honks do blare
    in beaten air

Of transcontinental crease

~Twelve~

I love you like a glacier
    carving through a mountain
I love you like the vapor
    flowing from a fountain

I love you like a deluge
    relentless on the roof
I love you like the vital need
    of Nile-dipped shadoof

I love you like the whispers
    of mist upon the skin
I love you like the trickle
    where the headwaters begin

I love you like a happenstantial
    spring among the sands
I love you like the shyness
    of slow determined hands

~Thirteen~

I love you like a morning mist
    Whose parted lips the meadow kissed

Who bedews lavender with amethyst
    And scents the air with ambergris

~Fourteen~

I love you like a marmoset
    vaulting through the trees

I love you like a devotee
    supplicate upon his knees

I love you like a blazing star
    at ten thousand degrees

I love you like the winter's
    white and wicked freeze

I love you from the acme of the A's
    to the zenith of the Z's

~Fifteen~

I love you like a chalice
    waiting to be brimmed

I love you like a pencil sketch
    meticulously limned

I love you like a thicket
    waiting to be trimmed

I love you like a cricket chorus
    joining with the hymned

~Sixteen~

I love you like the ocean breeze
    freshens up the room
I love you like the arid plain
    welcomes the monsoon

I love you like the cleansing
    of a timely cloudburst shower
I love you like a drop of dew
    magnifies the flower

I love you like blossoms
    decorate a pond
Like surface tension adheres
    dewdrops to a frond

I love you like a geyser
    unfulfilled and unrestrained
Old Faithful ever true
    dependable, maintained

~Seventeen~

I love you like an enchanted cellist
    bends on wooden bow
I love you like the silver strings
    of moon on river's flow

I love you like a hungry harpist
    devours every stroke
I love you like the strum of wind
    through ancient altar oak

I love you like a fervid flautist
    dances with her fingers
I love you like the aerophone arc
    of avian wings that lingers

I love you like a sexy saxophonist
    dips deep into the groove
And lifts it high like stillest reeds
    when blown, begin to move

~Eighteen~

I love you like a verdant crop
    fetched fresh from fields plowed

I love you like a raindrop from
    a rich and bulbous cloud

I love you like a fertile furrow
    a seedling's hope for height

I love you like a downy burrow
    a slumberer's delight

I love you like a nascent seed
    finds hope inside the loam

I love you like a heart welcomes
    another to its home

~Nineteen~

I love you like a tender shoot
    holding life by one lone root

Assured in its own pursuit
    to leaf and flower, frond and fruit

~Twenty~

I love you like a redwood
    ancient, thick and bold

Roots down deep in soil sleep
    tales left untold

Majestic as a soul can be
    the mighty, thick-skinned, soulful tree

Will tell its children of our love
    our tenderness, our glee

~Twenty-one~

I love you like eroded roots
    immersed in muddy river

I love you like saguaros
    awaiting cloud deliver

I love you like the Andean cacti
    collect the ocean dew

I love you like a forest peace
    provides an apercu

I love you like crescendo torrent
    on corrugated tin

I love you like the silence
    of the desert deep within

~Twenty-two~

I love you like the centuries
    have quantified our souls

I love you like a centaur
    merges two to make its wholes

I love you like the constant turn
    of ocean's shifting sands

I love you like the insistent burn
    of mighty Sol's demands

~Twenty-three~

I love you like a river thread
    woven into song

I love you like delivered bread
    to a hungry throng

I love you like a feather
    falling on a creek

I love you like the sweetest kiss
    upon your perfect cheek

~Twenty-four~

I love you like the distant stars
    accentuate the moon

I love you like a timber fire
    like torrential tide typhoon

I love you like a supernova
    releasing every mote

To cover your cartography
    in my kaleidoscopic cloak

I love you like the galaxies
    reveal the beyond

Like the melting of our hearts
    solidifies our bond

~Twenty-five~

I love you like a rain to drop
    I love you like a snow to flake

I love you like a tip to top
    I love you like a dawn to break

I love you like a be to bop
    I love you like a hip to shake

I love you like the cream to crop
    I love you like a mountain lake

~Twenty-six~

I love you like a butterfly
    dipping in the dew

I love you like an alligator
    slicing through the slough

I love you like the warmth
    of a heart-fed homemade stew

I love you like the winning card
    the only one I drew

~Twenty-seven~

I love you like a cottage
    is our perfect sylvan palace

I love you like the prismatic dance
    of the aurora borealis

I love you like an egret's feather
    caught up in the breeze

I love you like an errant kite
    titillates the trees

I love you like a river
    smoothing out the stones

I love you like the vibration
    of peace within our bones

~Twenty-eight~

I love you like the fervent breach
    and slow abatement of the waves

That thrusts our lives into the world
    and succors us to graves

And in between we find our gems
    scattered on the beach

Some we unearth with our toes
    for some we have to reach

~Twenty-nine~

I love you like a rogue sirocco
    stirring up the sands

Divulging and divesting
    relics from the lands

As if we need an overt
    Mother Earthly blast

To uncover what we predilect
    from promises of past

~Thirty~

I love you like the crispy sheets
    pulled up to my chin

I love you like the solar system's
    bright and balanced spin

I love you like the cozy blanket
    brushed upon my cheek

I love you like a crawdad finds
    refuge in the creek

I love you like the poem that lingers
    long and incites vision

I love you with the pulse of life
    a heart's devout decision

~Thirty-one~

I love you like the promise
    of the pond around the bend

The petals in a censer
    scented to transcend

The yearning of the heart to love
    be loved and mend

The calling of the spirit
    to my lifetimes-lover, dearest friend

Mischa Noel Revotskie
Aug 19, 1976 – Nov 19, 2020

Mischa was raised in rural Humboldt County, CA, the child of parents who were part of the back-to-land movement of the 1970s. He had two close companions, his twin sister, Shanti and nature. He graduated from high school as salutatorian and went on to UC Santa Cruz, obtaining his BA in Creative Writing. He drew inspiration from the beauty of nature around him in Santa Cruz, where he lived until his passing.

During his lifetime, Mischa became an accomplished disc golfer, competing in professional tournaments for many years. Mischa is also quite possibly the only one to ever have invented and played the "frisbee base," which is an impromptu musical instrument created by stretching thick rubber bands across a frisbee.

Mischa had a vast and all-inclusive heart and his kindness touched many lives. For the last decade he worked at Trader Joe's in Santa Cruz and could be found behind the register with a yellow daisy behind his ear held in place by his huge, curly afro. On his lunch break or after work, you'd find him on a bench overlooking Monterey Bay, working the day's *New York Times'* crossword or chatting with a friend.

In addition to crosswords, poetry, and disc golf, Mischa loved children, animals, cooking, and nature. Mostly, however, he will be remembered for his open and accepting heart.

Like the serenity of dewdrops
decorate a morning glade
Like the brilliant shatter shower
of a waterfall cascade
We are made of stardust
and return to where we're made
– Mischa Revotskie

www.ingramcontent.com/pod-product-compliance
Lightning Source LLC
Chambersburg PA
CBHW061204070526
44579CB00010B/124